PRACTICE QUESTIONS FOR UIPATH RPA ASSOCIATE CERTIFICATION - CASE BASED – LATEST EDITION

PRACTICE QUESTIONS FOR UIPATH CERTIFIED RPA ASSOCIATE CASE BASED

First edition. March 25, 2023.

ISBN: 979-8215020241

Written by Exam OG.

EXAM OG

Certificate Introduction:

Welcome to "PRACTICE QUESTIONS FOR UIPATH RPA ASSOCIATE CERTIFICATION - CASE BASED – LATEST EDITION". This book is designed to help you prepare for the UiPath RPA Associate Certification exam. The certification is an industry-standard recognition of your proficiency in using UiPath to automate business processes. It demonstrates that you have a solid understanding of UiPath components, features, and functionality.

This book provides you with a comprehensive collection of practice questions that simulate the real exam. The questions are designed to test your knowledge of the concepts covered in the exam, and are presented in a case-based format that reflects real-world scenarios. You will be able to practice your skills in a simulated environment, giving you the confidence you need to succeed in the actual exam.

The book covers a wide range of topics, including UiPath Studio, Orchestrator, variables, data types, control flow, activities, and more. Each question is accompanied by detailed explanations that help you understand the correct answer and reinforce your knowledge. Additionally, the book includes tips and tricks to help you optimize your exam performance.

Whether you are a beginner or an experienced UiPath user, this book will help you prepare for the UiPath RPA Associate Certification exam and advance your career in the field of Robotic Process Automation.

PRACTICE QUESTIONS

Question 1:

You are a developer working on an automation project in StudioX. You need to add a custom package to the project dependencies. How do you accomplish this?

A) Click on the Manage Packages button in the ribbon, search for the package, and install it. The installed dependency will be available only for the current project.

B) Right-click on the Dependencies category in the Project panel, select Remove Dependency, and then search for the custom package. Once found, select Install to add it to the project.

C) Hover over the dependency in the Project panel, and click on the Update icon image alt text next to the available version number. The package will be installed automatically.

Explanation:

Answer - A

To add dependencies to a project in StudioX, you need to click on the Manage Packages button in the ribbon, search for the package, and install it. The installed dependency will be available only for the current project. Option B is incorrect because it explains how to remove a dependency, not add it. Option C is incorrect because it explains how to update a dependency, not add a custom package.

Question 2:

Scenario: A software developer is creating a workflow that involves passing data between different parts of the project. She needs to use the Arguments panel to define and customize the arguments.

Which of the following is not an option for the Argument Type property?

A) Boolean

B) Int32

C) System.Data.DataTable

D) Float

E) Array of [T]

Explanation:

Answer - D

The options for the Argument Type property include Boolean, Int32, String, Object, System.Data.DataTable, and Array of [T], but not Float.

Question 3:

Which symbol replaces zero or more characters in a string?

A) Asterisk (*)

B) Question mark (?)

C) Exclamation mark (!)

D) At symbol (@)

Explanation:

Answer - A

In a string, the asterisk (*) symbol replaces zero or more characters. It is especially useful when dealing with selector attributes that change dynamically. In the given example, a wildcard was used to generate a selector for a Notepad window whose title changes depending on the .txt file opened with it.

Question 4:

Which of the following statements about assets in UiPath Orchestrator is true?

A) Assets can only store text values.

B) Asset values cannot be assigned on a per-account basis.

C) The Get Asset activity in Studio requests information about a specific asset based on AssetName.

D) Assets are not encrypted in the Orchestrator database by default

Explanation:

Answer - C

UiPath Orchestrator allows assets to store different types of values, such as text, bool, integer, and credential. Asset values can be assigned on a per-account basis or as a global value. The Get Asset and Get Credential activities in Studio allow you to retrieve information about a specific asset by providing its AssetName. All asset types are encrypted in the Orchestrator database by default.

Question 5:

While developing an automation project that extracts data from a random name generator website and saves it in an Excel spreadsheet, you face an issue with the selector of the Attach Browser container during execution. Which of the following steps should you take to catch and handle the exception?

A) Place the Invoke workflow activity in the Try section of a Try Catch activity and select UiPath.Core.SelectorNotFoundException in the Catches section.

B) Add an If activity to check if the browser is open or closed, and use an Open Browser activity in the Then section if the browser is closed.

C) Add a Message Box activity in the Finally section of the Try Catch activity to display a message when the exception is caught.

D) All of the above steps should be performed to catch and handle the exception.

Explanation:

Answer - D

In this scenario, you should follow all the mentioned steps to catch and handle the exception properly. To monitor for exceptions, include the Invoke Workflow activity in the Try section of a Try Catch activity. Select UiPath.Core.SelectorNotFoundException in the Catches section to catch the specific exception. Add a Message Box activity in the Catches section to inform the user about the exception. Use an If activity to check if the browser is open or closed, and open the browser using the Open Browser activity in the Then section if the browser is closed. This way, you can handle the exception and ensure the smooth execution of the automation project.

Question 6:

Which of the following steps correctly describes the process to add a Machine Template in Orchestrator?

A) Go to Tenant > Machines > Add machine > Add Standard Machine

B) Go to Tenant > Machines > Add machine > Machine template

C) Go to Tenant > Machines > Machine Template > Add machine

D) Go to Tenant > Machine Template > Machines > Add machine

Explanation:

Answer - B

In order to create a machine template, one must go to Tenant > Machines. On the Machines page, click Add machine > Machine template. This will display the Machine template page where you can configure the necessary settings for your new machine template.

Question 7:

An organization administrator wants to review the events linked to a specific tenant in their Orchestrator service. Where can they find this information?

A) Admin > Organization > Audit Logs

B) Orchestrator's Audit page

C) Automation Ops documentation

D) Robot logs at Orchestrator's folder level

Explanation:

Answer - B

The audit from the Orchestrator service lists all events linked to a specific tenant, such as folder or machine creations, package uploads, role assignments, and settings updates. To access this information, an

Administrator can go to the Orchestrator's Audit page. This page captures every step that may influence the orchestration process.

Question 8:

An RPA developer needs to create an automation for a virtualized environment such as a virtual machine or Citrix. Which UiPath Studio recording type should they use for this purpose?

A) Basic

B) Desktop

C) Web

D) Image

E) Native Citrix

Explanation:

Answer - D

UiPath Studio's Image recording type is tailored for recording virtualized environments, such as virtual machines, Citrix, VNC, and other similar environments. It is capable of only image, text, and keyboard automation and necessitates precise positioning. This recording type is suitable for the given scenario, as it targets virtualized environments.

Question 9:

A developer is working on an RPA project using UiPath Studio to iterate through a list of numbers. They want to stop the loop when the number 5 is encountered and then display the first, third, and fifth elements of the list. Which activity should they use inside the loop to achieve this?

A) Continue

B) Break

C) Terminate Workflow

D) Delay

Explanation:

Answer - B

The Break activity enables the loop to stop at a specific point and proceed with the subsequent activity. In this scenario, the developer can use the Break activity inside a For Each loop with a condition to stop when the number 5 is encountered. This allows the automation to continue with the next activity (displaying the first, third, and fifth elements of the list) after breaking out of the loop.

Question 10:

Automation developer is creating a new queue in Orchestrator for processing customer data. They need to make sure that the transaction references are unique and the queue items data and output are encrypted in the database. Which of the following options should the developer select when creating the queue?

A) Enforce unique references and Auto Retry

B) Store in encrypted format and Enforce unique references

C) Auto Retry and SLA Predictions

D) Schema Definitions and Store in encrypted format

Explanation:

Answer - B

To meet the requirements of the developer, they should select the "Enforce unique references" checkbox to make sure that transaction references are unique. They should also select the "Store in encrypted format" checkbox to ensure that the queue items data and output are encrypted in the database. The other options mentioned in the alternatives are not relevant to the given scenario.

Question 11:

Which of the following is NOT a type of recording option in UiPath?

A) Basic recording

B) Desktop recording

C) Web recording

D) Cloud recording

E) Citrix recording

Explanation:

Answer - D

UiPath offers various recording options, such as Basic recording, Desktop recording, Web recording, and Citrix recording. Basic recording focuses on automating single tasks, Desktop recording is used for various actions and application development, Web recording is used for viewing and recording web page activities, and Citrix recording is used for recording elements like images and virtualized environment automation. Cloud recording is not a type of recording option in UiPath.

Question 12:

You are an RPA developer working for an international company that recently hired a new team member from Japan. Your manager asked you to configure UiPath Studio to display the interface in Japanese for the new team member. How would you change the language settings for UiPath Studio?

A) Go to the Home (Studio Backstage View) and select "Japanese" from the list of languages.

B) Go to Settings > General and change the "Language" option to "Japanese."

C) Change the "Design Style" settings to "Japanese."

D) Go to Settings > Locations and set the "Language" option to "Japanese."

Explanation:

Answer - B

To change the interface language for UiPath Studio, go to the Home (Studio Backstage View), then navigate to Settings. Under the General settings tab, you will find the Language option where you can select "Japanese" from the available languages.

Question 13:

You are a UiPath developer working on a project for a client who requires detailed logging information for their RPA processes. They want to capture information about the activities, variables, and arguments used in the workflows. Which logging level should you set in UiPath Studio to meet the client's requirements?

A) Information

B) Warning

C) Error

D) Verbose

Explanation:

Answer - D

In UiPath, the Verbose logging level captures detailed information about activities, variables, and arguments used in the workflows. This includes execution start and end logs, transaction start and end logs, activity information logs, variable logs, and argument logs. The Verbose logging level provides the most comprehensive logging information compared to other logging levels, such as Information, Warning, and Error, which capture less detailed information.

Question 14:

You are an RPA developer using UiPath and have implemented a process that processes items from a queue in Orchestrator. Your manager asks you to generate a report on items that have been processed successfully, failed due to a business or application exception, and items that have been abandoned. Which item statuses should you include in the report?

A) New, In Progress, Failed

B) Successful, Failed, Abandoned

C) Successful, In Review, Verified

D) Retried, Deleted, None

Explanation:

Answer - B

When generating a report on items that have been processed successfully, failed due to a business or application exception, and items that have been abandoned, you should include the following item statuses:

Successful: After processing, the item was passed on to a Set Transaction Status activity, where its status was updated to Successful.

Failed: The item was transferred to the Set Transaction Status activity and had its status changed to Failed because it did not satisfy any business or application requirements within the project.

Abandoned: The item was in the In Progress status for an extended period of time (around 24 hours) without undergoing processing.

These three statuses are most relevant to your manager's request and will provide the necessary information about the processing results of the queue items.

Question 15:

Which keyboard shortcut enables you to step into a block of activities and execute the first one while debugging in UiPath Studio?

A) Ctrl + F11

B) Shift + F11

C) F11

D) F10

Explanation:

Answer - C

The F11 keyboard shortcut allows you to step into a block of activities and execute the first one while debugging in UiPath Studio. This feature is helpful for closely examining the execution of a specific block of activities during the debugging process.

Question 16:

You are an RPA developer and you need to create an automation that involves interacting with a Gmail account using UiPath Studio. Which of the following steps is NOT necessary for configuring the Gmail account for IMAP/POP3 protocols?

A) Enable POP3/IMAP from Gmail.

B) Generate and use a Google app password.

C) Disable 2-step verification for your Gmail account.

D) Access the Gmail Settings page.

Explanation:

Answer - C

In order to configure your Gmail account for IMAP/POP3 protocols and use it in your automations, you must enable POP3/IMAP from Gmail and, if you have 2-step verification enabled, generate and use a Google app password. Disabling 2-step verification is not necessary; in fact, generating a Google app password only works if you have 2-step verification enabled for your Gmail account. Accessing the Gmail Settings page is a part of the process of enabling POP3/IMAP from Gmail.

Question 17:

You are developing an RPA automation process using UiPath Studio, and you want to use a dynamic selector to click on different menu items in Notepad. Which of the following steps is NOT needed for creating a dynamic selector?

A) Indicating the target element on the screen.

B) Creating a variable for the dynamic attribute value.

C) Modifying the default value of the variable in the Variables panel.

D) Manually editing the selector in the Selector Editor to add the variable

Explanation:

Answer - D

Creating a dynamic selector in UiPath Studio involves the following steps: indicating the target element on the screen, creating a variable for the dynamic attribute value, and modifying the default value of the variable in the Variables panel as needed. When you right-click the attribute value in the Selector Editor and choose to create a variable, the variable is automatically added to the selector, and there is no need to manually edit the selector to add the variable.

Question 18:

You are working on a UiPath automation project that reads data from an Excel file and processes it. You want to use the Output Data Table activity to convert a DataTable object to a CSV format string. Which of the following properties of the Output Data Table activity should be set to store the CSV format string?

A) DisplayName

B) DataTable

C) Text

D) Private

Explanation:

Answer - C

To convert a DataTable object to a CSV format string in UiPath, the Output Data Table activity is used. The resulting string can be stored by setting the 'Text' property of the activity. The 'DisplayName' property is used to specify the name of the activity that will be displayed in the workflow. The 'DataTable' property is where the DataTable object to be written into a string is inputted. The 'Private' property can be used to determine whether or not variable and argument values should be logged at the Verbose level.

Question 19:

You are automating a process that reads data from an Excel file and stores it in a DataTable variable. Using the Read Range Workbook activity, you want to read data from a specific sheet and range, preserving the cell formatting and including the column headers. Which properties of the Read Range Workbook activity should be set or selected?

A) WorkbookPath, SheetName, Range, AddHeaders, PreserveFormat

B) WorkbookPath, SheetName, Range, DisplayName, Private

C) WorkbookPath, SheetName, AddHeaders, PreserveFormat, Private

D) WorkbookPath, SheetName, Range, Password, Private

Explanation:

Answer - A

To read data from a specific sheet and range, preserving the cell formatting and including the column headers, you should set the following properties of the Read Range Workbook activity:

WorkbookPath: The full path of the Excel spreadsheet that you want to use.

SheetName: The name of the sheet in which the range that you want to read is.

Range: Specifies the range of cells to be read.

AddHeaders: Select this checkbox to extract the column headers from the specified spreadsheet range.

PreserveFormat: Select this checkbox to keep the formatting of the cell that you want to read.

The DisplayName property is used to specify the display name of the activity, the Password property is used for the password of the Excel workbook (if necessary), and the Private property controls the logging of variable and argument values at the Verbose level.

Question 20:

Which keyboard shortcut is used to open the folder where Log files are stored in UiPath Studio?

A) Ctrl + Shift + N

B) Ctrl + L

C) Ctrl + O

D) Ctrl + S

Explanation:

Answer – B

The keyboard shortcut Ctrl + L is used to open the folder where Log files are stored in UiPath Studio.

Question 21:

You are working as an RPA developer and tasked with automating a process that requires iterating through a list of items and performing certain actions on each item. Which type of loop would be most suitable for this task in UiPath?

A) While loop

B) Do While loop

C) For Each loop

D) Flowchart loop

Explanation:

Answer – C

The For Each loop is the most suitable choice for this task because it is designed to iterate through a list of items one at a time, and perform certain actions on each item. While loops and Do While loops are more suitable for situations where actions need to be repeated based on a specific condition. Flowchart loops can be created by connecting a certain point in the workflow to an earlier execution one, but the For Each loop provides a more structured and easy-to-understand way of iterating through a list of items.

Question 22:

You are an RPA developer working on a project that requires extracting data from a single string that contains the name of an author and a list of bookstores where the author's books are available. The input string has the following format: "You searched for Author X. His books can be found at the following stores: Bookstore 1, Bookstore 2, Bookstore 3." Your task is to extract the author's name and the list of bookstores as separate variables. Which of the following actions would be most suitable for extracting the author's name in UiPath Studio?

A) Use the Split method on the input string, followed by the Substring method to isolate the author's name.

B) Use the Replace method on the input string to remove unwanted text, leaving only the author's name.

C) Use a For Each loop to iterate through the input string and identify the author's name.

D) Use a Regular Expression (Regex) to match the author's name pattern.

Explanation:

Answer – A

In the given scenario, using the Split method on the input string, followed by the Substring method, is the most suitable way to isolate the author's name. This approach allows you to separate the input string into distinct array items and then isolate the author's name from the relevant array item. Option B (Replace method) would require multiple replacements to get the desired result and is less efficient. Option C (For Each loop) is not a suitable choice for string manipulation. Option D (Regex) could be used to extract the author's name, but in this specific case, the Split and Substring methods are more straightforward and easier to implement.

Question 23:

Which of the following is true regarding the GenericValue variable in UiPath Studio?

A) GenericValue variables can only store text data.

B) GenericValue variables can store text, numbers, dates, and arrays.

C) GenericValue variables cannot be automatically converted to other types.

D) GenericValue variables are unique to programming languages other than UiPath Studio.

Explanation:

Answer – B

The GenericValue variable in UiPath Studio is a versatile variable type that can store different types of data, such as text, numbers, dates, and arrays. It can be converted to other types automatically to perform specific tasks. However, it is crucial to use these variables judiciously as their automatic conversion may not always be the correct choice for your project.

Question 24:

XYZ Inc. is a consulting firm that provides automation solutions to its clients. The firm uses UiPath Studio to create libraries that contain reusable components and activities, which can be installed as dependencies to workflows using the Package Manager.

What is a library in UiPath Studio?

A) A .nupkg file is a packaged set of one or more workflows represented by a reusable component activity in UiPath.

B) A collection of reusable components that are saved as .nupkg files, which can be installed as dependencies to workflows using Package Manager, is called a package.

C) A project or test automation project extracted as a library to be reused in other projects.

D) A folder in UiPath Studio where all the workflows and activities are saved.

Explanation:

Answer – B

In UiPath Studio, a library is a package that consists of multiple reusable components saved as .nupkg files, which can be installed as dependencies to workflows through Package Manager. You can create a library by accessing the Studio Backstage View, clicking on Start, and then selecting Library. In the library creation process, you will need to provide details such as the name, location, and description. Once created, the Project Panel will display a tree view with the Project folder, Dependencies, and the NewActivity.xaml, which contains the workflow. Each workflow file in a library is accessible as an activity in projects where the library is installed as a dependency.

Question 25:

What is the purpose of the UiPath.MicrosoftOffice365.Activities.Excel.SetRangeColor activity?

A) To create a new Excel file in Microsoft Office 365.

B) To read data from an Excel file in Microsoft Office 365.

C) To set the background color of a specified range in an Excel file in Microsoft Office 365.

D) To delete an Excel file in Microsoft Office 365.

Explanation:

Answer – C

The UiPath.MicrosoftOffice365.Activities.Excel.SetRangeColor activity facilitates the setting of background color for a specific range in a Microsoft Office 365 Excel file. This activity is included in the UiPath.MicrosoftOffice365.Activities package and leverages the Microsoft Graph Update range format API to enable this functionality. It accepts inputs for the background color of the designated range, the specific range that requires the new background color, the name of the sheet, and the DriveItem of the Excel document.

Question 26:

A company is planning to use UiPath Automation Cloud to build and run automations. They want to know where their business data will be stored.

Question: Where is the Automation Cloud organization data hosted for organizations created up to and including 11 May 2022?

A) In the region selected at signup

B) In a different region upon request to UiPath Support

C) Always in the European Union

D) In the optimal region for performance

Explanation:

Answer – C

For organizations created up to and including 11 May 2022, the Automation Cloud organization data is always hosted in the European Union. Users can contact Support to request to have their data moved to a different region if needed.

Question 27:

What software requirements are needed to access the UiPath Customer Portal?

A) A compatible browser and an installation of the Customer Portal software

B) An internet connection with TLS 1.2 and a compatible browser

C) A specific operating system and a compatible browser

D) An internet connection with TLS 1.0 and a compatible browser

Explanation:

Answer – B

The UiPath Customer Portal does not require any installation. The only software requirement is a compatible browser and an internet connection with TLS 1.2.

Question 28:

In which section of the Customer Portal can you request a quote for new licenses?

A) License section

B) Services section

C) Request Quote tab

D) Enterprise License Agreement Dashboard

Explanation:

Answer – C

The Request Quote tab allows you to request a quote for new licenses by choosing the SKUs and quantities that you wish to purchase from the UiPath product and services catalog. It displays the Shop Products portal where you can select from different product categories such as Services, Standalone licenses, Automation Cloud licenses, and On-Premises licenses. Customer Admin users have access, by default, to request a quote. Customer Regular users need to be granted permissions by their Customer Admin, to be able to request a quote.

Question 29:

Which security certificates does the Customer Portal have?

A) ISO only

B) SOC 2 only

C) Both ISO and SOC 2

D) No security certificates

Explanation:

Answer – C

Customer Portal has both ISO/IEC 27001:2013 certification and SOC 2 certification, so the correct answer is C. It also mentions that authentication for Customer Portal is performed via Auth0, and user credentials are never stored in Customer Portal.

Question 30:

John is an RPA developer who wants to publish an automation project to a custom NuGet feed. He wants to prevent a specific file from being included in the published package. Which of the following steps should John follow to achieve this?

A) Right-click the file in the Project panel and select Ignore from Publish

B) Right-click the file in the Project panel and select Make Private

C) Select Custom as the publishing option in the Publish window

D) Click Next in the Package Properties tab

Explanation:

Answer – A

John can exclude a specific file from being included in the published package by right-clicking the file in the Project panel and selecting the "Ignore from Publish" option. However, it is important to note that this option is not applicable to workflow files in library projects. Option B, on the other hand, is used to prevent a workflow file from being displayed as a reusable component in the Activities panel when the published library is installed in a project. Option C is not relevant to the task at hand, and Option D is the next step after entering package properties and not related to the question.

Question 31:

John is a UiPath developer who is working on a project with his team. They want to connect their project to a source control system to better manage their code and collaboration. John tries to connect their project to both TFS and SVN, but it doesn't work. What should he do?

A) Connect to TFS and SVN at the same time

B) Connect only to TFS

C) Connect only to SVN

D) Connect to TFS first, then SVN later

Explanation:

Answer – B

It is not possible to connect to both TFS and SVN at the same time. Therefore, John should choose either TFS or SVN to connect their project to. In this case, since he has already tried connecting to both TFS and SVN, he should choose to connect only to TFS.

Question 32:

You are developing a workflow file for a financial application that involves multiple decision points and conditional branching. You want to choose the best layout diagram to represent this workflow.

Question: Which layout diagram is best suited for showcasing decision points within a process, especially when there are multiple conditions and branches to consider?

A) Sequence

B) Flowchart

C) State Machine

D) Global Exception Handler

Explanation:

Answer – B

Flowcharts provide greater flexibility in connecting activities and tend to represent a workflow in a simple two-dimensional layout. They are best suited for showcasing decision points within a process, especially when there are multiple conditions and branches to consider. In the scenario provided, the financial application involves multiple decision points and conditional branching, making the flowchart layout the best choice.

Question 33:

You work in a finance department and spend a lot of time manually updating data in various Excel sheets. You have a basic technical know-how and can work with Microsoft Excel proficiently. You want to automate this repetitive task to save time and increase efficiency.

Question: Which automation tool is recommended for you to automate this task?

A. UiPath Studio

B. UiPath StudioX

C. UiPath Orchestrator

D. UiPath Assistant

Explanation:

Answer – B

StudioX is designed to enable users without coding experience to automate their own repetitive tasks. If you have basic technical know-how, such as proficiency in Microsoft Excel, StudioX may be the right automation tool for you. It is recommended for automating repetitive tasks involving Microsoft Office, like common tasks you perform in Excel, Word, or PowerPoint.

Question 34:

A business owner wants to automate a process to extract data from a website and store it in a CSV file. They have basic technical knowledge and are familiar with UiPath Studio.

What is the first step to create a new UiPath project for web scraping?

A) Launch UiPath Assistant

B) Open UiPath Studio and click on "Process" in the HOME Backstage view

C) Install the required UiPath extension in your browser

D) Create a new CSV file to store the scraped data

Explanation:

Answer – B

The first step to create a new UiPath project for web scraping is to open UiPath Studio and click on "Process" in the HOME Backstage view. From there, you can create a new project, name it, and select its location. Then, you can use the Activities panel to add the necessary activities for web scraping, such as "Use Application/Browser," "Get Text," and "Write CSV."

Question 35:

John works for a global organization that uses UiPath products to automate its business processes. He is responsible for implementing and maintaining the automation workflows in his region. John wants to know which UiPath products are available in his native language, Spanish.

Which of the following languages is not supported for Automation Suite in the current release?

A) Chinese (Simplified)

B) Chinese (Traditional)

C) French

D) German

Explanation:

Answer – B

Traditional Chinese support for Automation Suite is expected with the 2023.4 release.

Question 36:

Which type of account is used for running back-office unattended processes that should not be the responsibility of any particular user?

A) Local account

B) Directory account

C) Robot account

D) Service account

Explanation:

Answer – C

Robot accounts are used to run back-office unattended processes that should not be the responsibility of any particular user. They are non-user identities with permissions similar to user accounts, and can be added and managed by organization administrators from the Admin > Accounts & Groups page. Robot accounts are not allowed to configure interactive-related processes and do not require an email address to be created.

Question 37:

Sarah is a developer working on a UiPath project that involves managing queues. She wants to create a new queue for the project. What is the maximum number of characters allowed for the queue name and queue description respectively?

A) 50 and 500

B) 250 and 500

C) 50 and 250

D) 500 and 50

Explanation:

Answer – C

The maximum value for the queue name is 50 characters, and the maximum value for the queue description is 250 characters. Therefore, option C is correct. Options A, B, and D are incorrect as they provide incorrect information regarding the maximum number of characters allowed for the queue name and description.

Question 38:

In Orchestrator, what should you do to create an asset with a unique reference and specific per-account values?

A) Enable the "Global Value" toggle and provide a default value for the asset

B) Add robot asset values for all accounts that require a specific value

C) Select "Credential" as the type of asset and enter a username and password in the "Value" field

D) Choose "Integer" as the type of asset and add per-account values using the "Add robot asset value" button

Explanation:

Answer – B

To create an asset with specific per-account values, you must disable the "Global Value" toggle and use the "Add robot asset value" button to add the desired values on a per-account basis. The other options provided in the MCQ are incorrect: enabling the "Global Value" toggle will provide a default value for the asset, but it will not allow for specific per-account values; selecting "Credential" as the type of asset and entering a username and password in the "Value" field is only relevant for credential assets and does not pertain to unique references; and choosing "Integer" as the type of asset is not necessary for unique references and does not allow for specific per-account values.

Question 39:

A company has recently implemented UiPath automation to manage their customer service requests. The automation uses Orchestrator and queues to manage incoming requests. The team wants to add a new customer service request to the queue using the UiPath.Core.Activities.AddTransactionItem activity.

Question: What does the UiPath.Core.Activities.AddTransactionItem activity do?

A) Adds a new item to the queue and sets the status to InProgress, returning the item as a QueueItem variable.

B) Retrieves information about queues, items, and statuses from Orchestrator.

C) Connects the robot to Orchestrator in order to send and retrieve information about queues, items, and statuses.

D) Creates a new folder in Orchestrator and adds a new transaction item to the folder.

Explanation:

Answer – A

When you use the UiPath.Core.Activities.AddTransactionItem activity, a new item is added to the queue and a transaction is initiated, setting the item status to InProgress. After that, the activity returns the item in the form of a QueueItem variable, which you can use in other automation steps that follow. This activity is used when a new item needs to be added to the queue, such as a new customer service request in the scenario provided.

Question 40:

A company has recently implemented UiPath automation to manage their customer service requests. The automation uses Orchestrator and queues to manage incoming requests. The team wants to add a new customer service request to the queue using the UiPath.Core.Activities.AddTransactionItem activity.

Question: What does the UiPath.Core.Activities.AddTransactionItem activity do?

A) Adds a new item to the queue and sets the status to InProgress, returning the item as a QueueItem variable.

B) Retrieves information about queues, items, and statuses from Orchestrator.

C) Connects the robot to Orchestrator in order to send and retrieve information about queues, items, and statuses.

D) Creates a new folder in Orchestrator and adds a new transaction item to the folder.

Explanation:

Answer – A

The UiPath.Core.Activities.AddTransactionItem activity is designed to add a new item to the queue and begin a transaction, with the status of the item set to InProgress. Upon completion, the activity returns the added item as a QueueItem variable, which can be utilized in subsequent automation steps. This activity is commonly employed when there is a need to add a new item to the queue, such as a new customer service request in the scenario given.

Question 41:

ABC company has a process that needs to run every day at 5:00 pm. They have three robots available in the environment. The process needs to run 10 times in one go. The company also wants to ensure that the process doesn't run during non-working days. What is the best way for ABC company to configure their trigger?

A) Set up a time trigger to run at 5:00 pm every day and allocate dynamically to all available robots. Use the Non-Working Days feature to define non-business days and ensure that the trigger doesn't run during those days.

B) Set up a queue trigger and set the Minimum number of items to trigger the first job to 10. Allocate the jobs dynamically to all available robots. Use the Non-Working Days feature to define non-business days and ensure that the trigger doesn't run during those days.

C) Set up a time trigger to run at 5:00 pm every day and select Specific Robots to run the job. Use the Non-Working Days feature to define non-business days and ensure that the trigger doesn't run during those days.

D) Set up a queue trigger and set the Minimum number of items to trigger the first job to 10. Select Specific Robots to run the job. Use the Non-Working Days feature to define non-business days and ensure that the trigger doesn't run during those days.

Explanation:

Answer – A

Option A is the best way for ABC company to configure their trigger because they need to run the process at a specific time every day and allocate the jobs dynamically to all available robots to utilize resources to their greatest extent. They also want to ensure that the trigger doesn't run during non-working days, which can be achieved by using the Non-Working Days feature. Option B, C, and D are not suitable because they either do not allocate the jobs dynamically or do not run the process at the required time or do not use the Non-Working Days feature.

Question 42:

You are working on a project in UiPath Studio and need to create a variable that will store a person's name. You want to make sure that the variable is only available in a specific activity and has a default value set.

Question:

What is the purpose of the Variables panel in UiPath Studio?

A) To enable you to create workflows

B) To enable you to create and modify variables

C) To enable you to execute jobs at regular intervals

D) To enable you to create queue triggers

Explanation:

Answer – B

The Variables panel in UiPath Studio enables you to create variables and modify them. Variables are used to store information in a workflow and can be of different types, such as Boolean, Int32, String, Object, Generic Value, or Array of [T]. The Variables panel allows you to set the variable type, name, scope, and default value. By default, variables are available in the entire project, but you can specify a specific activity or scope for the variable.

Question 43:

You are a developer working on a project that requires the use of variables in UiPath Studio. You need to create a variable to store employee names in a specific activity.

Question: Which type of variable should you use to store employee names in UiPath Studio?

A) Boolean

B) Int32

C) String

D) Object

Explanation:

Answer – C

String type variables are used to store text-based information such as employee names, usernames or any other strings. Therefore, to store employee names in a variable in UiPath Studio, you should use a String type variable.

Question 44:

A software developer is working on a project in UiPath Studio and has created multiple variables to store different types of data. Now, he wants to remove some of the variables that are no longer needed. How can he remove variables in UiPath Studio?

Which of the following options is correct for removing a variable in UiPath Studio?

A) Variables can only be removed from the Variables panel

B) Variables can only be removed from the Data Manager

C) Variables can be removed from both the Variables panel and the Data Manager

D) Variables can be removed by pressing the Backspace key when the cursor is on the variable

Explanation:

Answer – C

Both the Variables panel and the Data Manager allow variables to be removed. In the Data Manager, the *Variables node must be expanded, and then right-click on a variable and select Delete Variable, or select the variable and press the Delete key. In the Variables panel, right-click on a variable and select Delete or select the variable and press the

Delete key. The Studio ribbon also provides an option to remove all variables that are defined but not used in the current file. Select Remove Unused > Variables, then click Yes to confirm.

Question 45:

What is the recommended naming convention for variables?

A) Random names

B) Descriptive and accurate names

C) Abbreviated names

D) Similar names

Explanation:

Answer – B

It is recommended to use descriptive and accurate names for variables to easily identify the information the variable stores. It is also recommended to use Camel Case for better readability.

Question 46:

What are the different types of variables that can be created in UiPath Studio?

A) Boolean, Int32, String, Object, System.Data.DataTable, Array of [T], and Browse for Types

B) Only Boolean, Int32, and String

C) Only String and System.Data.DataTable

D) Only Object and Array of [T]

Explanation:

Answer – A

In UiPath Studio, you have the option to create variables of various types such as Boolean, Int32, String, Object, System.Data.DataTable, Array of [T], and Browse for Types. The value stored within a variable can be of multiple types depending on the variable type. Boolean type variables can have two possible values - true or false. Int32 type variables are used for storing numeric information. String type variables are used to store text information. Object type variables can hold different types of data. System.Data.DataTable type variables can store large pieces of information and can act as a database or a simple spreadsheet with rows and columns. Array of [T] variables allow you to store multiple values of the same type. By selecting the Browse for Types option, you can explore more types that are relevant to your task.

Question 47:

Sarah is an RPA developer who is creating an automation to automate a process in a legacy system. She wants to identify the elements on the UI and generate selectors to use in her automation. However, she is unsure whether to use full selectors or partial selectors.

Question:

What is the difference between full selectors and partial selectors in UiPath?

A) Full selectors contain all the elements needed to identify a UI element, while partial selectors do not contain information about the top-level window.

B) Full selectors are generated by the Desktop recorder, while partial selectors are generated by the Basic recorder.

C) Full selectors are recommended when performing multiple actions in the same window, while partial selectors are recommended when switching between multiple windows.

D) Full selectors are editable in Selector Editor and UI Explorer, while partial selectors are not.

Explanation:

Answer – A

Full selectors provide complete details for identifying a UI element on the screen and include information about the top-level window. They are created by the Basic recorder and are useful when working with multiple windows. In contrast, partial selectors are generated by the Desktop recorder and do not include information about the top-level window. They are recommended when working within the same window for multiple actions. The Selector Editor and UI Explorer display the full selector, but only the elements belonging to the partial selector can be modified.

Question 48:

Which of the following statements about UIExplorer is true?

A) UIExplorer is a feature available only in the UiPath.UIAutomation.Activities package.

B) UIExplorer is a standalone tool that requires you to install Studio.

C) UIExplorer allows you to create a custom selector for a specific UI element.

D) UIExplorer displays a tree of the UI hierarchy and enables you to navigate through it, by clicking the arrows in front of each node.

Explanation:

Answer – C

UIExplorer is a sophisticated tool that lets you generate a personalized selector for a particular UI element. It is available as a standalone application that can be downloaded from the Resource Center in your Automation Cloud instance or from Studio, but only if the UiPath.UIAutomation.Activities package is installed as a project dependency. You don't need to install Studio if you use UI Explorer as a standalone tool, which is useful if you want to verify whether an application can be automated with selectors. The standalone package also includes the SetupExtensions utility, which allows you to install browser extensions and the JavaBridge, so you can inspect elements for all your automation needs.

Question 49:

You are working on a project that involves automating a Windows application with multiple windows. You have noticed that some of the activities in your automation project are using partial selectors, while others are using full selectors. You are wondering which type of selector is recommended in each scenario.

Question:

When is it recommended to use a full selector instead of a partial selector?

A) When performing multiple actions in the same window

B) When switching between multiple windows

C) When the UI element is nested within another element

D) When the UI element has a dynamically changing attribute value

Explanation:

Answer – B

When identifying a UI element, full selectors are generated by the Basic recorder and include all the information necessary, including the top-level window. They are suitable when switching between multiple windows. In contrast, partial selectors, generated by the Desktop recorder, do not have top-level window information. However, activities with partial selectors are enclosed in a container, such as Attach Browser or Attach Window, that has a full selector of the top-level window. Partial selectors are recommended when performing multiple actions in the same window. To summarize, use a full selector when switching between multiple windows, and use a partial selector when performing multiple actions in the same window.

Question 50:

A software company has recently released a new version of their product, and as part of the QA testing process, you are required to create an automation process that opens the Help menu and clicks on a specific item, using a dynamic selector.

Question: What is a dynamic selector?

A) A selector that only contains information about the top-level window.

B) A selector that contains all the elements needed to identify a UI element.

C) A selector that uses a variable or an argument as a property for the attribute of your target tag.

D) A selector that is generated by the Desktop recorder.

Explanation:

Answer – C

In order to identify a target element, a dynamic selector uses a variable or argument as a property for the attribute of the target tag. This allows the selector to adapt to changing values of the variable or argument, instead of relying on an exact string that may change due to interactions within the automation project. As a result, the variable or argument can be modified to interact with a different element without having to modify the selector.

Question 51:

John is working on an automation project and needs to create a custom selector for a specific UI element. Which tool can he use to achieve this?

A) UI Automation Libraries

B) UiPath.UIAutomation.Activities package

C) UI Explorer

D) Visual Tree Panel

Explanation:

Answer – C

UI Explorer is an advanced tool that allows you to generate a custom selector for a particular UI element. You can access it as a standalone tool by downloading it from the Resource Center in your Automation Cloud instance, or through Studio if the UiPath.UIAutomation.Activities package is installed as a project dependency.

Question 52:

John, a software developer, wants to create an automation that extracts data from a large dataset. He needs to use a loop to go through all the records in the dataset and extract relevant information. He decides to use the Do While activity to accomplish this task.

Question: What is the purpose of the Do While activity in John's automation?

A) To execute the automation repeatedly until a specified condition is met

B) To execute a particular activity multiple times

C) To browse through array indices

D) To exit the loop when a specified condition is no longer met

Explanation:

Answer – A

The Do While activity allows you to repeatedly execute a designated portion of your automation as long as a condition remains true. This activity is especially handy for iterating through all the elements of an array or executing a specific task multiple times. In John's case, he needs to use the Do While activity to go through all the records in the dataset and extract relevant information, which requires executing the automation repeatedly until all records have been processed.

Question 53:

A company has a large database of customer information and they want to automate a process that extracts data from the database and saves it to a file. They also want to stop the process once a specific condition is met. Which activity would you use in this scenario?

A) Assign activity

B) Break activity

C) Do While activity

D) For Each activity

Explanation:

Answer – C

In the given scenario, the Do While activity is the most suitable option as it allows the process to continue as long as a certain condition is met, and it exits the loop when that condition is no longer met. This is useful when the company wants to extract data from the database and save it to a file until a specific condition is met, and then stop the process.

The Assign activity allows you to assign a value to a variable, which is not useful in this scenario. The Break activity allows you to stop the loop at a chosen point and continue with the next activity, but it can only be used within one of the following activities: For Each, While, or Do While. Finally, the For Each activity is useful when you want to iterate over a collection of items and perform an action on each item. However, it is not the best option in this scenario as the condition for stopping the loop is not related to iterating over a collection of items.

Question 54:

A developer is designing a state machine workflow in UiPath Studio. They want to create a transition between two states and set a condition for the transition. Which of the following statements is true regarding the Transition activity?

A) The Transition activity can be found in the Activities Panel and dragged onto the workflow canvas.

B) The Transition activity is generated automatically when a State is linked to another State or a Final State.

C) The Transition activity accepts any Boolean variable as a condition for the transition.

D) Line breaks are allowed in the condition expression of the Transition activity.

Explanation:

Answer – B

The Transition activity cannot be dragged from the Activities Panel like a conventional activity. It is generated automatically when you link a State to another State or to a Final State. Therefore, option A is incorrect. The Transition activity can only accept Activity<Boolean> variables as a condition for the transition, making option C incorrect. Line breaks are not supported in the condition expression of the Transition activity, making option D incorrect. Thus, the correct answer is B.

Question 55:

A developer is creating an automation project in UiPath Studio and wants to set up a Global Exception Handler for the project. Which of the following statements is true regarding the Global Exception Handler?

A) The Global Exception Handler can be set for both processes and library projects.

B) The Global Exception Handler has only one argument, errorInfo, which stores information about the error that was thrown.

C) The result argument of the Global Exception Handler determines the level of the error to be logged in the Log Message activity.

D) The Global Exception Handler retries an activity an unlimited number of times before aborting with an error message.

Explanation:

Answer – A

The Global Exception Handler is only available for processes and not for library projects, making option A correct. The Global Exception Handler has two arguments, errorInfo and result, and both should not be removed, making option B incorrect. The errorInfo argument stores information about the error that was thrown and the workflow that failed, while the result argument determines the next behavior of the process when it encounters an error, including whether to continue, ignore, retry, or abort, making option C incorrect. The Global Exception Handler retries an activity three times before aborting with an error message, making option D incorrect. Thus, the correct answer is A.

Question 56:

John is a UiPath developer and he needs to create a new process. Which keyboard shortcut should he use?

A) Ctrl + Shift + N

B) Ctrl + O

C) Ctrl + S

D) Ctrl + Shift + S

Explanation:

Answer – A

The shortcut Ctrl + Shift + N creates a new Blank Process, which is exactly what John needs to do. Option B, Ctrl + O, is used to open a previously created workflow. Option C, Ctrl + S, is used to save the currently opened workflow, and Option D, Ctrl + Shift + S, is used to save all the workflows that are currently open.

Question 57:

A company has a large database of customer information and needs to remove a column from their customer data table. They want to use UiPath to automate this process.

Question: Which property of the Remove Data Column activity is used to specify the DataTable object from which the column is to be removed?

A) ColumnIndex

B) ColumnName

C) Column

D) DataTable

Explanation:

Answer – D

The DataTable property is used to specify the DataTable object from which the column is to be removed. The ColumnIndex property specifies the index of the column to be removed, the ColumnName property specifies the name of the column to be removed, and the Column property specifies a DataColumn object to be removed.

Question 58:

In a software development project, a developer wants to determine the length of a string input in a user interface. Which function should they use?

A) Count

B) Size

C) Length

D) Dimension

Explanation:

Answer – C

The Length function is used to determine the number of characters contained in a text type input. In the given scenario, the developer wants to determine the length of a string input in a user interface, so the appropriate function to use is the Length function. The Count function is used to count the number of elements in a collection, and the Size function is used to determine the size of a file or a data type in memory. The Dimension function is not a built-in function in most programming languages.

Question 59:

You are developing a UiPath automation process to extract email addresses from a list of contacts. However, the email addresses in the list are in different formats such as john.doe@example.com, johndoe@example.com, john.doe@example.co.in, etc. How can you use RegEx search to identify all email addresses in the list?

A) Use the following selector to identify all email addresses:

```
<webctrl tag='a'
href='regex:(?i)[A-Z0-9._%+-]+@[A-Z0-9.-]+\.[A-Z]{2,}(\.[A-Z]{2,})?'
/>
```

B) Use the following selector to identify all email addresses:

```
<webctrl tag='a'
href='matching:href=^[A-Za-z0-9._%+-]+@[A-Za-z0-9.-]+\.[A-Za-z]{2,4}$'
/>
```

C) Use the following selector to identify all email addresses:

```
<webctrl tag='a'
href='regex:[a-zA-Z0-9._%+-]+@[a-zA-Z0-9.-]+\.[a-zA-Z]{2,4}' />
```

D) Use the following selector to identify all email addresses:

```
<webctrl tag='a'
href='matching:href=[a-zA-Z0-9._%+-]+@[a-zA-Z0-9.-]+\.[a-zA-Z]{2,4}'
/>
```

Explanation:

Answer – C

In this scenario, RegEx search can be used to identify all email addresses in the list by searching for the pattern of email addresses. The regular expression used to match email addresses is [a-zA-Z0-9.%+-]+@[a-zA-Z0-9.-]+.[a-zA-Z]{2,4}, which checks for one or more characters before the "@" symbol, followed by one or more characters after the "@" symbol, a period (".") and two to four letters at the end. Therefore, the correct selector to identify all email addresses is the one that uses the regex:[a-zA-Z0-9.%+-]+@[a-zA-Z0-9.-]+.[a-zA-Z]{2,4} attribute to apply the regular expression pattern to the href attribute of the <webctrl> tag. Option C is the correct answer.

Question 60:

A financial institution needs to process loan applications from multiple customers. The details of each customer and their loan application are stored in a DataTable. The institution needs to loop through each row in the DataTable and perform certain actions for each row, such as calculating the loan amount and updating the customer's account status.

Question: What is the purpose of the For Each Row in Data Table activity in this scenario?

A) To create a new DataTable variable for each row in the input DataTable

B) To execute a set of actions once for each row in the input DataTable

C) To sort the input DataTable by a specific column

D) To update the data type of a column in the input DataTable

Explanation:

Answer – B

The For Each Row in Data Table activity allows the automation to loop through each row in the input DataTable and perform certain actions for each row. The Item property can be used to reference the current row in the contained activities. This activity is useful when dealing with large amounts of data that need to be processed or manipulated in some way. In the given scenario, the automation can use this activity to loop through each row in the DataTable and perform the necessary calculations and updates to the customer's account status.

Question 61:

John is working on a project and needs to extract data from a CSV file. He wants to use UiPath to automate the process. Which activity should he use to read all the entries from the CSV file?

Options:

A) RemoveDataColumn

B) RegEx Search

C) For Each Row in Data Table

D) ReadCsvFile

Explanation:

Answer – D

The ReadCsvFile activity is used to read all the entries from a specified CSV file. It has properties such as FilePath, Delimiter, Encoding, Has headers, and Output DataTable. The activity allows the user to extract data from CSV files and store it in a DataTable variable. In the given scenario, John wants to extract data from a CSV file, hence he should use the ReadCsvFile activity to achieve the desired outcome. Option A, B, and C are not related to CSV file data extraction.

Question 62:

A company needs to automate their invoice processing system. They have a lot of PDF invoices received from various vendors, which need to be converted into structured data to enter into their accounting system. They decide to use OCR technology to extract the required data from the invoices.

Question: What is the property in the Get OCR Text activity that specifies the timeout duration before the SelectorNotFoundException error is thrown?

A) Output

B) Target.Selector

C) Target.TimeoutMS

D) Target.WaitForReady

Explanation:

Answer – C

The Target.TimeoutMS property of the Get OCR Text activity specifies the amount of time (in milliseconds) to wait for the activity to run before the SelectorNotFoundException error is thrown. This property allows the activity to wait for a specific amount of time before throwing an error, in case the OCR screen scraping method is unable to extract the required text within the specified time.

Question 63:

A company needs to automate their invoice processing system. They have a lot of PDF invoices received from various vendors, which need to be converted into structured data to enter into their accounting system. They decide to use OCR technology to extract the required data from the invoices.

Question: Which property of the Get OCR Text activity specifies the amount of time to wait for the activity to run before the SelectorNotFoundException error is thrown?

A) Output

B) Target.Selector

C) Target.TimeoutMS

D) Target.WaitForReady

Explanation:

Answer – C

The Target.TimeoutMS property of the Get OCR Text activity specifies the amount of time (in milliseconds) to wait for the activity to run before the SelectorNotFoundException error is thrown. This property allows the activity to wait for a specific amount of time before throwing an error, in case the OCR screen scraping method is unable to extract the required text within the specified time.

Question 64:

You work for a large insurance company and your job is to extract policy information from various documents submitted by customers. These documents come in different formats, including PDF, Word, and image files. Your task is to extract relevant policy information such as policy number, policy holder name, coverage details, and premium amount from these documents and store them in a database for further processing.

You decide to use UiPath Studio to automate the data extraction process. You use the Screen Scraping Wizard to identify the UI elements containing the required information, and select the OCR method for extracting text from image files.

To ensure accuracy and completeness of the extracted information, you use the Native method for extracting text from PDF and Word files. You also use the Get Words Info option to get the screen coordinates of each word found in the UI elements. This allows you to identify and extract relevant information even if the formatting of the document changes.

To handle different file formats and ensure that the extracted data is stored in a structured manner, you use the Read PDF, Read Text, and Read OCR Text activities. These activities allow you to extract data from PDF, Word, and image files respectively, and store the extracted data in a DataTable variable.

You also use the Get Attribute activity to extract additional information such as the date of the policy, and the Get Ancestor activity to identify the policy holder's contact information from the document.

Finally, you use the Write Range activity to store the extracted information in an Excel spreadsheet, which can be easily accessed and processed by other teams within the company.

Which activity allows you to extract additional information such as the date of the policy?

A) Get Ancestor

B) Get Attribute

C) Get Position

D) Screen Scraping Wizard

Explanation:

Answer – B

The Get Attribute activity allows you to extract the value of a specified UI element attribute, such as the date of the policy.

Question 65:

A financial analyst wants to extract data from multiple PDF files containing company financial reports. However, some of the PDF files are scanned copies, and the analyst needs to extract the data from those as well. Which activity would be best for this task?

A) Read PDF Text

B) Read PDF With OCR

C) Screen Scraping

D) Get OCR Text

Explanation:

Answer – B

The Read PDF With OCR activity uses OCR technology to extract characters from PDF files, including scanned copies. The other options (Read PDF Text, Screen Scraping, and Get OCR Text) do not use OCR technology and may not be able to extract data from scanned PDF files. Therefore, the best activity for this task would be Read PDF With OCR.

Question 66:

You are working on an automation project that requires data to be copied from an existing Excel file and pasted into a new Excel file. You need to use the Append Range activity to ensure that the new data is added after the existing data in the new Excel file.

Question:

What is the Append Range activity used for?

A) To create a new table or range in an Excel file.

B) To copy data from an Excel file and paste it into another application.

C) To copy data from a table, range, or sheet in an Excel file and paste it after existing data in another table, range, or sheet.

D) To edit data in an Excel file.

Explanation:

Answer – C

The Append Range activity is used to copy data from a table, range, or sheet in an Excel file and paste it after existing data in another table, range, or sheet. This activity can be used with Excel files selected for parent Use Excel File activities or with the Project Notebook. The data can be copied as values, formulas, number and cell formats, and can be transposed. The Append Range activity is helpful in automating tasks that require adding new data to an existing Excel file.

Question 67:

A customer service representative at a call center is required to verify customer information by checking the customer's ID card. The ID card has a unique identification number that needs to be entered into the company's database. However, the number on the card is not always in a consistent location, and it can vary from one card to another. The customer service representative wants to automate this process by using

OCR technology to read the ID card number and input it into the database.

Question: What is the purpose of the OCR Text Exists activity in this scenario?

A) To check if the customer's ID card has a unique identification number.

B) To search for the location of the ID card number using OCR technology.

C) To read the ID card number from the UI element or image using OCR technology.

D) To input the ID card number into the company's database.

Explanation:

Answer – B

The OCR Text Exists activity is used to search for a specific text in a given UI element or image using OCR technology. In this scenario, the OCR Text Exists activity can be used to search for the location of the ID card number on the customer's ID card. Once the location is found, the OCR technology can be used to read the number and input it into the company's database. Therefore, the correct answer is b) to search for the location of the ID card number using OCR technology.

Question 68:

In which scenario can the Clear Data Table activity be useful?

A) When you want to add data to a DataTable

B) When you want to remove specific rows from a DataTable

C) When you want to remove all data from a DataTable

D) When you want to update data in a DataTable

Explanation:

Answer – C

The Clear Data Table activity is useful when you want to remove all data from a DataTable. It clears all the data in the specified DataTable. Option A is incorrect because adding data to a DataTable requires the use of the Add Data Row or Add Data Column activities. Option B is incorrect because removing specific rows from a DataTable requires the use of the Remove Data Row activity. Option D is incorrect because updating data in a DataTable requires the use of the Assign activity to modify the value of a specific cell in the DataTable.

Question 69:

You are working as a UiPath developer for a company that uses an attended robot to automate a process that extracts data from various websites. The robot is set up to run the process daily at a specific time. One day, you notice that the robot did not run the process at the scheduled time. You check Orchestrator and find that the job is in a "pending" state. What does this mean?

A) The robot has established a connection to the designated website and is currently running the process.

B) The robot failed to start or the process threw an unhandled error during execution.

C) The job is queued on the robot, but it has not established a connection yet.

D) The robot stopped executing the process before it finished without throwing any errors.

Explanation:

Answer – C

The "pending" state means that the job is queued on the robot, but it has not established a connection yet. It could be waiting for other jobs to finish or it could be trying to establish a connection with the robot. Once the connection is established, the job will move to the "running" state.

Question 70:

A company is using UiPath Orchestrator to manage the automation processes for their financial department. They have several attended and unattended robots. The company has recently hired a new employee who needs to learn about jobs and how to start them in Orchestrator.

Question:

Which of the following statements is correct regarding jobs in UiPath Orchestrator?

A) Jobs can only be launched from Orchestrator on attended robots.

B) Jobs can only be launched from Orchestrator on unattended robots.

C) Jobs can be launched from Orchestrator on both attended and unattended robots.

D) Jobs can be launched from UiPath Assistant or the Robot Command Line Interface.

Explanation:

Answer – C

Launching jobs from Orchestrator can be done in both attended and unattended mode. Attended jobs can also be triggered from UiPath Assistant or the Robot Command Line Interface. Unattended jobs can be launched from Orchestrator directly from the Jobs or Processes page or through triggers on the Triggers page. Therefore, the correct answer is option D, but it is not complete as it does not mention the possibility of launching jobs from the Jobs or Processes page. Option A is incorrect because jobs can be launched on unattended robots as well. Option B is also incorrect because jobs can be launched on both attended and unattended robots.

Question 71:

A robot is processing a queue of invoices to be paid, and one of the items in the queue has failed due to an application exception. What will be the status of this item?

A) In Progress

B) Failed

C) Successful

D) Abandoned

Explanation:

Answer – B

If an item in the queue fails due to an application or business exception, its status will be changed to Failed. The Set Transaction Status activity is responsible for changing the status of a failed item. This allows the reviewer to know that there was an issue with the item and that it needs to be reviewed. Additionally, the history of changes made to the item will be recorded in the History tab of the Audit Details window.

Question 72:

A company is developing a process automation for its HR department. They need to capture and store the names of new employees in a variable for future use. They want to display the first name of the employee in the output panel. Which activity should they use?

A) Input Dialog

B) Assign

C) Write Line

D) None of the above

Explanation:

Answer – A

In order to capture and store the names of new employees, the Input Dialog activity should be used. The activity will prompt the user to input the full name of the employee, which can be stored in a string variable. The FirstLetter variable can be created using the Assign activity and the Substring() function, which will capture the first letter of the full name. Finally, the Write Line activity can be used to display the first letter of the employee's name in the output panel.

Question 73:

A developer is working on an automation project that requires gathering information from a web page and writing it to an Excel spreadsheet. The automation uses an Invoke Workflow activity to read the web data, but sometimes the browser window fails to open, leading to a SelectorNotFoundException.

Question: What is the purpose of the Try Catch activity in the provided scenario?

A) To create a new Excel spreadsheet.

B) To read data from a web page.

C) To catch an exception when the browser window fails to open.

D) To close Internet Explorer.

Explanation:

Answer – C

The Try Catch activity is used in the provided scenario to catch the SelectorNotFoundException that occurs when the browser window fails to open during the web data reading process. This helps to prevent the automation from failing and allows the developer to handle the exception in a more controlled way, such as displaying a message to the user or attempting to open the browser window again. Options A, B, and D are not the main purpose of the Try Catch activity in this scenario.

Question 74:

A developer is trying to debug a project in UiPath Studio, but they keep encountering an error when trying to start the debugging process. What could be the reason for this issue?

A) The project contains validation errors.

B) The developer is using the wrong keyboard shortcut for Step Into.

C) The Slow Step feature is causing the debugging process to fail.

D) The developer has not enabled Picture in Picture mode.

Explanation:

Answer – A

The debugging process is not available if project files have validation errors. Therefore, if the developer encounters an error when trying to start the debugging process, the first thing they should check is whether there are any validation errors in the project files. Options B, C, and D are not relevant to this issue.

Question 75:

You are debugging an automation process and have reached a section where a database query is being executed. However, the query seems to be returning incorrect data. You suspect that the issue is with the query itself, and you need to debug it to identify the problem.

Which debugging action would be most helpful in this situation?

A) Step Over

B) Step Into

C) Step Out

D) Slow Step

Explanation:

Answer – B

Step Into is the most helpful debugging action in this situation because it allows you to debug activities one at a time, and in this case, you can debug the database query activity to identify the issue with the query.

When Step Into is used with activities that involve database operations, the query can be viewed and analyzed step by step, which can be very useful in identifying issues with the query.

Option A) Step Over is used for skipping analysis of large containers which are unlikely to trigger any issues during execution, so it wouldn't be as helpful in this situation.

Option C) Step Out is used for stepping out and pausing the execution at the level of the current container. This option works well with nested sequences, but it wouldn't be as helpful in debugging a database query.

Option D) Slow Step is used to take a closer look at any activity during debugging, but it wouldn't be as helpful in this situation where the focus is on identifying issues with the database query.

Question 76:

Sophia is a UiPath developer who needs to create a library for her team to reuse in multiple processes. She wants to know how to create a library and how to manage reusable component activities.

Which of the following is true about Libraries in UiPath?

A) Libraries are saved as .xml files and can be installed as dependencies to workflows using Package Manager.

B) Libraries are packages which contain multiple reusable components and are saved as .nupkg files that can be installed as dependencies to workflows using Package Manager.

C) Libraries are reusable components activities that represent one or more workflows packaged together as a .nupkg file, and utilized in other processes.

D) Libraries are used to create test automation projects to use its templates in other automation projects.

Explanation:

Answer – B

In UiPath, libraries are collections of reusable components that are packaged as .nupkg files and can be installed as dependencies using the Package Manager. These components consist of one or more workflows packaged together as a single .nupkg file and can be used in other processes for increased reusability. Therefore, option B is the correct answer. Option A is incorrect because Libraries are saved as .nupkg files, not .xml files. Option C is not completely true as it defines reusable component activities, which are a part of Libraries, but not the entire definition. Option D is also incorrect as Libraries are not used to create test automation projects to use its templates in other automation projects.

Question 77:

A company is interested in using UiPath software for commercial purposes. They want to have access to premium features and are willing to pay for it. Which licensing plan should they choose?

A) Community

B) Free

C) Pro Trial

D) Pro

E) Enterprise

Explanation:

Answer – D

The Pro plan grants access to premium features at the platform level and is available for purchase online, with the option to cancel at any time. The Enterprise plan is a yearly plan that includes custom license types and counts tailored to specific needs with help from the Sales team, and is generally more suitable for larger companies with complex automation needs. The Free plan provides basic development and attended automation capabilities, but it is limited in terms of licenses and functionality. The Pro Trial plan is only for evaluation purposes and has a limited time frame of 60 days. The Community plan is intended for non-commercial use only and is not suitable for companies looking for premium features.

Question 78:

A small company is interested in implementing UiPath automation software for their business processes. They have limited resources and want to start with the most basic capabilities.

Question: Which licensing plan is best suited for the small company in the scenario above?

A) Community plan

B) Free plan

C) Pro Trial plan

D) Pro plan

Explanation:

Answer – A

The Community plan is the most basic licensing plan and provides instant access to elementary automation capabilities through licenses for users and UiPath services. It is also free and aimed at non-commercial use. The Free plan, Pro Trial plan, and Pro plan provide more advanced capabilities, but at a cost. Since the small company in the scenario has limited resources and wants to start with the most basic capabilities, the Community plan is the best fit for their needs.

Question 79:

Alice has been using UiPath Studio 2021.2 Community edition and wants to update to the latest stable release. What should she do?

A) Wait for the automatic update to happen

B) Manually update the Studio from the Resource Center in UiPath Automation Cloud

C) Use the 32-bit version of the installer to update existing installations on 32-bit operating systems

D) Use the 64-bit version of the installer to update existing 32-bit and 64-bit installations on 64-bit operating systems.

Explanation:

Answer – A

Alice is using the Community edition of UiPath Studio, she activated it with a Community license, Studio and Robot are automatically updated as soon as a new version is available on the selected channel, Stable or Preview. Therefore, the best option for her is to wait for the automatic update to happen. Option B is incorrect because it is for the Enterprise edition and involves downloading the installation artifacts from the Resource Center in UiPath Automation Cloud, which is not applicable to the Community edition. Option C is also incorrect because Alice is using the 64-bit operating system, and Using the 64-bit version of the installer to update existing 32-bit and 64-bit installations on 64-bit operating systems. Option D is incorrect because Alice is not using the 32-bit operating system, so using the 64-bit version of the installer is the correct choice.

Question 80:

What is the minimum recommended CPU for running one robot?

A) 2 x 1.8GHz 32-bit (x86)

B) 4 x 2.4GHz 64-bit (x64)

C) 8 GB RAM

D) 3.5 GB disk space

Explanation:

Answer – A

The minimum recommended CPU for running one robot is 2 x 1.8GHz 32-bit (x86). This is the minimum requirement and might not be enough for more complex workflows or additional software installed on the machine, which could affect the robot's performance.

Question 81:

A team of developers is working on a large automation project. They are required to pass data between different workflows and are looking for a way to manage the arguments efficiently.

How can unused arguments be removed from a workflow in UiPath?

A) By right-clicking the argument in the Arguments panel and selecting Delete

B) By selecting Remove Unused > Arguments in the Studio ribbon and confirming

C) By selecting Delete in the context menu of the Data Manager

D) Both b and c

Explanation:

Answer – D

Unused arguments can be removed from a workflow in UiPath by selecting Remove Unused > Arguments in the Studio ribbon and confirming or by selecting Delete in the context menu of the Data Manager.

Question 82:

A company uses UiPath to automate its invoice processing. The process involves multiple workflows passing data between each other. The project manager has noticed that some of the arguments are not being used and wants to remove them to reduce clutter.

Which of the following argument types are supported by UiPath?

A) Integer, Double, Float

B) String, Boolean, Object, Array, DataTable

C) Char, Long, Short

D) Dictionary, Set, Queue, Stack

Explanation:

Answer – B

UiPath provides support for a wide range of argument types that correspond to the various types of variables. Some of the commonly used argument types include Generic Value, String, Boolean, Object, Array, or DataTable. Additionally, users can also browse for .Net types similar to the way they browse for variables.

Question 83:

Sarah is a software developer who is working on a project that involves gathering information from users and displaying it in a message box. She decides to use sequences in UiPath for this task.

What is one of the key features of sequences in UiPath?

A) They can only be used as a standalone automation

B) They cannot be reused in different settings

C) They can only be used as part of a flowchart

D) They can be reused time and again, as a standalone automation or as part of a state machine or flowchart

Explanation:

Answer – D

Sequences have a key feature that enables them to be reused multiple times, either as a standalone automation or as a component of a flowchart or state machine.

Question 84:

You work for a logistics company that delivers goods to customers. You need to create an automation that will help the delivery team manage their routes efficiently. The automation will use a state machine to manage the delivery process and ensure that each delivery is completed on time.

Task:

Create a state machine automation that will manage the delivery process for the logistics company.

Requirements:

The automation must use a state machine to manage the delivery process.

The initial state should prompt the user to input the delivery addresses.

The next state should generate a delivery route based on the delivery addresses entered in the initial state.

The next state should prompt the user to confirm the delivery route and start the delivery process.

The next state should mark each delivery as completed as it is made.

The final state should display a message indicating that all deliveries have been completed.

What is the purpose of the state that prompts the user to confirm the delivery route?

A) To generate a delivery route

B) To mark each delivery as completed

C) To prompt the user to confirm the delivery route and start the delivery process

D) None of the above

Explanation:

Answer – C

The state that prompts the user to confirm the delivery route ensures that the delivery team is ready to begin the delivery process.

Question 85:

You are working on an automation project for a financial institution that involves processing large amounts of data. You need to use VBScript to perform some calculations and generate a report. You have a VBScript file saved on your computer that contains the necessary code for the task.

Which activity should you use to execute the VBScript file in UiPath?

A) Invoke Code activity

B) Invoke PowerShell activity

C) Invoke VBA activity

D) Invoke VBScript activity

Explanation:

Answer – D

The Invoke VBScript activity in UiPath is specifically designed to execute VBScript files. The other options listed, such as Invoke Code, Invoke PowerShell, and Invoke VBA, are used for executing other types of code. Therefore, the correct answer is D.

Question 86:

A company is processing invoices for its clients and needs to automate the data extraction process from the scanned invoices. However, the invoices come in different formats, making it difficult to use normal scraping or UI automation technologies. The company decides to use OCR-based activities in UiPath Studio to scan the invoices and extract the required information.

What are OCR-based activities in UiPath Studio used for?

A) To automate virtual machine environments

B) To scrape data from web pages

C) To scan the entire screen of the machine, finding all the characters that are displayed

D) To automate normal UI selectors

Explanation:

Answer – C

UiPath Studio provides OCR-based activities that allow scanning the entire screen of the machine to detect all the displayed characters. With OCR-based activities, users can create automations based on the on-screen content, which simplifies automation in virtual machine environments or in situations where normal UI selectors are hard to identify.

Question 87:

A company wants to create a data table to store customer information such as name, address, phone number, and email. They want to use UiPath's Build Data Table activity to create this data table.

Question: Which of the following fields can be edited when adding a new column using the Build Data Table activity?

A) Column Name

B) Data Type

C) Allow Null

D) All of the above

Explanation:

Answer – D

When utilizing the Build Data Table activity to add a new column, various fields can be customized, including Column Name, Data Type, Allow Null, Auto Increment, Default Value, Unique, and MaxLength. The Column Name field specifies the name of the column and only accepts string values. The Data Type field designates the type of values the column can contain. Selecting Allow Null permits null values to be added to the column's rows. By selecting Auto Increment and setting the Data Type to Int32, the column's value is automatically incremented by 1 each time a new row is added. Default Value denotes the default value of all rows that are added to the column. If Unique is chosen, all rows within the column must have unique values. MaxLength refers to the maximum number of characters allowed in the column, and if no maximum is specified, the default value of -1 is applied.

Question 88:

As an RPA developer, you need to add a new item in an Orchestrator queue. You want to specify the deadline, priority, and reference for the queue item. Which properties of the UiPath.Core.Activities.AddQueueItem activity should you use?

A) Deadline, Priority, and Reference

B) Item Information, Postpone, and Folder Path

C) Queue Name, Deadline, and Item Collection

D) Folder Path, Item Information, and Private

Explanation:

Answer – A

To specify the deadline, priority, and reference for a queue item, you should use the Deadline, Priority, and Reference properties of the UiPath.Core.Activities.AddQueueItem activity, respectively. The Item Information property is a collection of additional information about the queue item, and the Postpone property is used to specify the date after which the queue item may be processed. The Folder Path property is used to specify the path of the folder where the specified queue is located, and the Private property is used to prevent the values of variables and arguments from being logged at Verbose level. Thus, options B, C, and D are incorrect.

Question 89:

A company wants to securely store their Amazon login credentials in an Orchestrator asset and use them in their automation process in UiPath Studio. They want to use the Get Credential activity to retrieve the credentials.

What is the first step in using the Get Credential activity in UiPath Studio?

A) Create a SecureString variable to store the password

B) Create a String variable to store the username

C) Create a Credential asset in Orchestrator

D) Drag the Get Credential activity to the Main panel

Explanation:

Answer – C

The first step in using the Get Credential activity is to create a Credential asset in Orchestrator. The asset should store the username and password for the Amazon login. After that, in UiPath Studio, a String variable should be created to store the username, and a SecureString variable to store the password. Then, the Get Credential activity should be dragged to the Main panel, and the name of the Credential asset should be entered in the AssetName field in the Properties panel, along with the variables created for the username and password.

Question 90:

John is a developer who has created a workflow that extracts data from an email and saves it to a database. He is concerned that the workflow might be interrupted by a user or administrator stopping the job in Orchestrator. To handle this situation, he decides to add the Should Stop activity to the workflow.

Question: What is the purpose of the Should Stop activity?

A) It extracts data from an email and saves it to a database.

B) It checks if somebody stopped a running job using the Stop option in UiPath Orchestrator.

C) It performs a clean-up routine to close windows and applications which have been targeted within the workflow.

D) It informs users that the job was stopped in Orchestrator.

Explanation:

Answer – B

The Should Stop activity in UiPath is used to determine if a running job has been stopped through the Stop option in UiPath Orchestrator. It helps to ensure a seamless termination of a job, preventing any abrupt interruption of an ongoing process. Additionally, it provides the ability to configure the workflow to execute various routines after the stop is triggered. For instance, in the given scenario, John decides to add the Should Stop activity to his workflow to handle the situation where he is concerned about potential interruptions.

Question 91:

John works as a UiPath developer in a company and wants to update his Studio version to the latest one. He has installed the Community Edition and activated it with a Community license.

Question: How does John update his Community Edition Studio to the latest version?

A) He needs to download the installation artifacts from the Resource Center in UiPath Automation Cloud and perform a manual update.

B) Studio and Robot are automatically updated as soon as a new version is available on the selected channel, Stable or Preview.

C) He needs to select Update now in the Update Available notification displayed by the UiPath Update Agent to perform the update.

D) He needs to go to Home (Studio Backstage View) > Help and select either Stable or Preview to choose an update channel.

Explanation:

Answer – B

Once John has installed Studio and Robot using the Community Edition installer and activated it with a Community license, any new versions of Studio and Robot are automatically updated as soon as they become available on the chosen channel, either Stable or Preview. Therefore, he doesn't need to perform a manual update, select Update now in the Update Available notification, or choose an update channel.

Question 92:

Jane is a UiPath developer and wants to automate a Java application. She is using Java 11 and Windows 10 Enterprise edition. Which of the following statements is true regarding the UiPath Extension for Java?

A) The UiPath Extension for Java is not compatible with Java 11.

B) The UiPath Extension for Java will work on Jane's Windows 10 Enterprise edition with applications opened with Java JRE.

C) Jane can install the UiPath Extension for Java using the ScreenScrapeJavaSupport tool.

D) If Jane installs the UiPath Extension for Java when prompted by UI Explorer, the Java Bridge files will be deployed only in the JDK directory.

Explanation:

Answer – B

The UiPath Extension for Java can be used with any version of JRE's, from Java 3 to Java 17, including Java 11. However, when it comes to Java 9 and above, the UiPath Extension for Java only works on Windows Enterprise and non-Enterprise editions with applications opened with Java JDK. If the applications are opened with Java JRE, the UiPath Extension for Java can only be used on non-Enterprise Windows editions. This means that option B is correct. While option

A is incorrect, options C and D contain some elements of truth, but they are not directly related to the scenario presented.

Question 93:

Emily and John are both developers working on a Studio automation project. They need to collaborate on the project and keep track of changes made to the code. They decide to use a source control system to help them manage the project.

Question:

Which of the following source control systems can be connected to Studio automation projects?

A) GIT and TFS

B) SVN and TFS

C) GIT, SVN, and TFS

D) None of the above

Explanation:

Answer – C

Studio automation projects can be linked to source control systems such as GIT, SVN, or TFS. This can be done by navigating to Home (Studio Backstage View) > Team. It is worth noting that only one source control system can be connected to Studio at a time. The GIT, SVN, and TFS source control plugins are enabled by default in Studio, but can be enabled or disabled individually by going to Home (Studio Backstage View) > Tools > Plugins. While working on a project in Studio, the Add to Source Control button located in the status bar provides quick access to GIT Init, Copy to GIT, Add to TFS, and Add to SVN.

Question 94:

What are the minimum requirements for accessing UiPath Automation Cloud?

A) An internet connection with TLS and a compatible web browser

B) A compatible operating system and internet connection with TLS

C) A compatible web browser and UiPath Robot

D) A compatible web browser and UiPath Studio

Explanation:

Answer – A

To access UiPath Automation Cloud, a compatible web browser and an internet connection with TLS are the minimum requirements. The supported browsers and their minimum versions for compatibility with Automation Cloud are listed in a table in the documentation. It is important to note that browsers not listed in the table, older versions of the supported browsers, and mobile browsers are not supported.

Question 95:

You are working on a project that involves automating data entry into multiple windows of an application. You need to select the appropriate selector type for each activity in your workflow to ensure successful automation.

Question: Which selector type is recommended when switching between multiple windows in an application?

A) Partial selector

B) Full selector

C) Both partial and full selectors can be used interchangeably

D) None of the above

Explanation:

Answer – B

Complete selectors are selectors that include all the information necessary to identify a UI element, including the top-level window. They are useful when switching between multiple windows in an application. In contrast, partial selectors are useful when performing multiple actions in the same window, as they do not contain information about the top-level window.

Question 96:

John is a software developer who is working on an automation project. He is using UI Explorer to create a custom selector for a specific UI element. Which of the following statements is true regarding UI Explorer?

Which of the following statements is true regarding UI Explorer?

A) UI Explorer is a standalone tool that requires UiPath.UIAutomation.Activities package installed as a dependency for the project to work.

B) UI Explorer is a tool used to build processes, but it is not possible to inspect elements without building a process.

C) UI Explorer does not support browser extensions and JavaBridge.

D) UI Explorer is used to create both full and partial selectors.

Explanation:

Answer – A

The UiPath UI Explorer is a separate tool that can be obtained by downloading it from the Resource Center within your Automation Cloud instance. It operates independently of UiPath Studio and provides the ability to examine elements without constructing an automation project. To function correctly, the tool necessitates the UiPath.UIAutomation.Activities package installed as a project dependency. The tool also includes the SetupExtensions utility, which allows you to install browser extensions and the JavaBridge, allowing you to examine elements in all of your automation tasks. Therefore, option A is the correct answer. Option B is incorrect because UI Explorer is not just used to build processes. Option C is incorrect because UI Explorer does support browser extensions and JavaBridge. Option D is incorrect because UI Explorer is used to create custom selectors, which can be both full and partial, but it is not used to create full or partial selectors themselves.

Question 97:

John is a beginner level RPA developer and he wants to create an automation that takes an input number from the user and checks whether it's odd or even. Based on the value, it should output a different message to the Output panel.

Which activity should John use to achieve this functionality?

A) For Each

B) Switch

C) If

D) While

Explanation:

Answer – A

The Switch activity is explained as a tool to select one choice out of multiple based on the value of a specified expression. In the scenario given, John wants to check if the input number is odd or even and based on that, output a different message. Switch activity can be useful for this purpose as it allows to categorize data according to a custom number of cases.

Option A) For Each activity is used to iterate through an array or collection of items.

Option C) If activity is used to create conditional statements and allows the automation to take different paths based on whether the condition is true or false.

Option D) While activity is used to repeatedly execute a set of activities while a specified condition is true.

Therefore, the correct answer is B) Switch.

Question 98:

Maria wants to create an automation that extracts data from a list of employees in her company's database. She wants to iterate through each employee and process their information individually. Which activity should she use?

A) If activity

B) Switch activity

C) For Each activity

D) While activity

Explanation:

Answer – C

By utilizing the For Each activity, you can navigate through various types of collections such as arrays, data tables, and lists, in order to execute operations on each element of the collection individually. This allows for the processing of information in a streamlined and organized manner. In this case, Maria wants to iterate through a list of employees and process their information, so the For Each activity is the best choice for her.

Question 99:

A company wants to create an automation project that asks for the user's email address and displays the domain name in the Output panel. Which type of variable should be used to store the email address?

A) Integer

B) Boolean

C) Text or String

D) Array

Explanation:

Answer – C

To store the user's email address, a text or string variable should be used. Text or string variables can store any string of characters, including email addresses. Once the email address is stored in the variable, the domain name can be extracted and displayed using string manipulation functions. Integer and boolean variables are not suitable for storing email addresses, as they are designed to store numerical values and true/false values, respectively. Arrays can be used to store multiple email addresses, but a single email address can be stored in a text or string variable.

Question 100:

Sarah wants to retrieve text from a UI element in a virtual environment. However, she cannot find the selector for the target element. Which of the following techniques can she use to retrieve the text?

A) OCR technology

B) Selector identification

C) Screen capturing

D) Image recognition activities

Explanation:

Answer – A

In situations where selectors cannot be found, OCR technology can be used to retrieve text from UI elements. This is called Relative Scraping, and it uses image recognition activities to look for adjacent labels or other elements as anchors to identify the location of the target element.

Question 101:

You are working on an automation project that requires searching for a specific text in an image or UI element using OCR technology. Which activity should you use?

A) Click Image

B) Find Text Position

C) OCR Text Exists

D) Get OCR Text

Explanation:

Answer – C

OCR Text Exists is the activity that checks if a text is found in a given UI element or image by using OCR technology. It has properties such as Text, Occurrence, Target.Element, and Target.ClippingRegion. The output is a Boolean variable that indicates if the text exists or not. Click Image is used to simulate the click on a specified image. Find Text Position is used to find the position of a specified text in an image. Get OCR Text is used to retrieve the text from a specified UI element or image using OCR technology.

Question 102:

Which of the following activities can be used to change the status of a transaction item in a queue to "Successful" or "Failed"?

A) Get Transaction Item

B) Set Transaction Status

C) Add Queue Item

D) Add Transaction Item

Explanation:

Answer – B

The Set Transaction Status activity can be used to change the status of a transaction item in a queue to "Successful" or "Failed". In UiPath,

Application Exceptions should be handled when the application being automated fails, while Business Exceptions should be raised when a particular queue item does not meet the business requirements. The Get Transaction Item activity is used to retrieve an item from the queue and sets its status to In Progress for processing. The Add Queue Item activity is used to add items to the queue and define a deadline for processing them. Lastly, the Add Transaction Item activity is used to add an item to the queue, start the transaction and set its status to In Progress.

Question 103:

You are working as an automation developer for a financial firm that deals with loans. Your manager has asked you to populate a specific queue with loan applications data that is stored in a CSV file. You need to use the "ProcessAllIndependently" strategy for uploading the data, and also map the custom headers to the "Specific Data" section in Orchestrator. Which of the following is true regarding column mapping when uploading a CSV file to Orchestrator queue using a predefined column header?

A) The Reference column is mapped to the Specific Data section, instead of the Reference column.

B) Numeric data greater than 253 or less than -253 are converted to Integer to preserve precision.

C) The Deadline column must be populated with a date in the following format: YYYY-MM-DD.

D) The Priority column is uploaded with a low priority by default if not specified in the file.

Explanation:

Answer – C

When uploading a CSV file to an Orchestrator queue using a predefined column header, the Deadline column must be populated with a date in one of the following formats: YYYY-MM-DD, YYYY/MM/DD, YYYY MM DD, YYYY-MM-DD HH:mm, YYYY/MM/DD HH:mm, YYYY MM DD HH:mm, YYYY-MM-DD HH:mm:ss, YYYY/MM/DD HH:mm:ss, or YYYY MM DD HH:mm:ss. The Reference column is mapped to the Reference column, not the Specific Data section. Numeric data greater than 253 or less than -253 are not converted to Integer to preserve precision. If the Priority column is not specified in the file, the items are uploaded with a high priority by default.

Question 104:

What are the two upload strategies available for bulk uploading queue items using a CSV file in Orchestrator?

A) AllOrNothing and AllInOne

B) ProcessAllIndependently and DownloadFailed

C) ProcessAllIndependently and AllOrNothing

D) ProcessOneByOne and UploadFailed

Explanation:

Answer – C

When bulk uploading queue items using a CSV file in Orchestrator, there are two upload strategies available: ProcessAllIndependently and AllOrNothing. The ProcessAllIndependently strategy handles each item individually, and if it is processed successfully, adds it to the queue. If an item cannot be processed, it will be listed in a file containing the same fields as in the initially uploaded file. This file can be downloaded in CSV format. On the other hand, the AllOrNothing strategy adds all the items to the queue only if all of them are processed successfully. If any item fails to process, none of the items are added.

Question 105:

A company is using UiPath to automate their invoice processing system. The process reads invoices from a queue in Orchestrator and performs necessary actions. The company wants to update the status of a particular transaction item in the queue as Failed if it cannot be processed. Which activity should they use to accomplish this task?

A) Get Queue Item activity

B) Add Queue Item activity

C) Set Transaction Status activity

D) Get Transaction Item activity

Explanation:

Answer – C

The Set Transaction Status activity is used to set the status of an Orchestrator transaction item to Failed or Successful. In this scenario, the company can use this activity to update the status of a particular transaction item in the queue as Failed if it cannot be processed. This helps to maintain the accuracy of the queue by marking the failed transaction as such, and prevents the same transaction item from being processed again.

Question 106:

Which of the following methods can be used to activate UiPath Studio?

A) Signing in to your UiPath account

B) Connecting to Orchestrator with your client credentials or machine key

C) Adding a license key

D) All of the above

Explanation:

Answer – D

The UiPath Studio can be activated using any of the following methods:

Signing in to your UiPath account

Connecting to Orchestrator with your client credentials or machine key

Adding a license key

The activation method presented to you during the installation process is dependent on the type of installation you have chosen. However, you have the option to switch to a different activation method by selecting "More Options" in the installation wizard.

Question 107:

ABC Corp is interested in trying out UiPath products for free. They want to know which licensing plan they should choose to match their automation needs and budget. Which licensing plan would be appropriate for them?

A) Free plan

B) Community plan

C) Pro Trial plan

D) Enterprise plan

Explanation:

Answer – A

The Free plan gives users instant access to basic development and attended automation capabilities, which can be used for commercial purposes. This plan is suitable for those who want to try out UiPath products for free and match their automation needs and budget. As ABC Corp is interested in trying out UiPath products for free, the Free plan would be the appropriate choice for them.

Question 108:

A user wants to create a new process using UiPath Studio. Which shortcut should the user use?

A) Ctrl + Shift + N

B) Ctrl + O

C) Ctrl + L

D) Ctrl + S

Explanation:

Answer – A

The keyboard shortcut Ctrl + Shift + N is used to create a new Blank Process in UiPath Studio. Option B, Ctrl + O is used to open a previously created workflow. Option C, Ctrl + L is used to open the folder where the Log files are stored. Option D, Ctrl + S is used to save the currently opened workflow.

Question 109:

You are a developer working on a project for UI Path. Your team is creating an automated test case for the UI Bank web application. The test case is called "Data-Driven Loan". You need to attach a data source to the test case to make it a data-driven test case.

What are the options for attaching a data source to a data-driven test case in Studio Pro?

A) Select the data source that's already part of your project or attach an excel file that is not part of your project.

B) Attach a PDF file to the test case.

C) Only attach an excel file that is already part of your project.

D) There is no option to attach a data source to a data-driven test case in Studio Pro.

Explanation:

Answer – A

There are two options to attach a data source to a data-driven test case in Studio Pro. You can either select the data source that's already part of your project or attach an excel file that is not part of your project. This allows you to create a data-driven test case that processes different data through your web application, without redundancy in your automation.

Question 110:

Which of the following best describes an array variable in UiPath Studio?

A) A variable that stores multiple values of different types.

B) A variable that enables you to store only one value of the same type.

C) A variable that enables you to store multiple values of the same type.

D) A variable that enables you to store values of different types in a single array.

Explanation:

Answer – C

Using an array variable in UiPath Studio allows for storing multiple values of the same type. UiPath Studio supports various types of arrays, the same as it supports types of variables, meaning you can create an array of numbers, strings, booleans, and more. The example provided shows how an array of string variables, called NameAge, is utilized to store multiple values of the string type.

Question 111:

You are building an automation project that will calculate the total cost of a customer order. You need to pass some data from one activity to another activity within the project. Which of the following should you use?

A) Variables

B) Arguments

C) Data Tables

D) Objects

Explanation:

Answer – B

Arguments are used to pass data from one activity to another activity within a project. In contrast, variables pass data between activities, while arguments pass data between automations. In this scenario, you need to pass data from one activity to another activity within the project, so arguments are the appropriate option. Variables are useful for storing data within a single activity or across multiple activities within a single automation, while data tables are used to store large amounts of structured data, and objects are used to represent real-world entities.

Question 112:

You are working on a project that requires a delay of 10 seconds between two activities. Which activity would you use to implement the delay in the project?

A) Delay

B) Write Line

C) Input Dialog

D) Assign

Explanation:

Answer – A

The Delay activity is used to pause the automation for a custom period of time. In this scenario, we need to delay the execution of the second activity by 10 seconds, and we can achieve this by adding a Delay activity between the two activities with a duration of 10 seconds.

Therefore, option A is the correct answer. Option B, C, and D are not relevant to implementing the delay in the project.

Question 113:

Which activity enables you to skip the remaining steps in the current iteration inside a loop activity?

A. Delay

B. Continue / Skip Current

C. If

D. Switch

Explanation:

Answer – B

The UiPath.Core.Activities.Continue activity enables you to skip the remaining steps in the current iteration inside a loop activity, such as For Each, While, or Do While loop. This activity is useful when you need to stop processing the current item and move on to the next one. In the StudioX profile, this activity is named Skip Current. The other options, Delay, If, and Switch, are not related to skipping iterations in a loop.

Question 114:

Which activity in UiPath Studio enables the user to reload the web page currently displayed in the specified browser?

A) Refresh Browser

B) Reload Page

C) Reinitialize Browser

D) Restart Browser

Explanation:

Answer – A

The RefreshBrowser activity in UiPath Studio allows the user to reload the web page that is currently displayed in the specified browser. It has a single input property, the Browser variable, which specifies the browser to be refreshed. The activity can be found under the UiPath.Core.Activities namespace. It is useful in situations where the automation is interacting with a website or web application and needs to reload the page due to some change in the web content or user input.

Question 115:

Which activity can be used to create an image from a specific page in a PDF file?

A) UiPath.PDF.Activities.PDF.ExtractPDFData

B) UiPath.PDF.Activities.PDF.ExportPDFPageAsImage

C) UiPath.PDF.Activities.PDF.MergePDFFiles

D) UiPath.PDF.Activities.PDF.SplitPDFFile

Explanation:

Answer – B

The ExportPDFPageAsImage activity can be used to create an image from a page in a specified PDF file. It has properties such as FileName, OutputFileName, Password, ImageDpi, and PageNumber that allow you to customize the image creation process. The supported image extensions are .png, .jpeg, .tiff, .bmp, and .gif.

Question 116:

Which of the following statements best describes UiPath Orchestrator?

A) A web application that enables you to manage your entire robot fleet and orchestrate repetitive business processes.

B) A software that allows launching of robots in unattended automation only.

C) A tool that is used for creating and maintaining connection between robots.

D) A tool that is used for storing and indexing the logs to a CSV database.

Explanation:

Answer – A

UiPath Orchestrator is a web application that allows users to manage their entire robot fleet and orchestrate repetitive business processes. It provides various capabilities such as provisioning, deployment, configuration, queues, monitoring, logging, and inter-connectivity. Orchestrator plays a vital role in managing the delivery and execution of automation packages by robots. It ensures centralized management of package versions in attended automation and delivers them to robots for execution. For unattended automation, Orchestrator enables the immediate launch of unattended execution or its pre-planned setup with triggers.

Question 117:

Which of the following statements about UiPath Orchestrator is true?

A) It is a desktop application for managing robots.

B) It is used to extract structured data from browsers, applications or documents.

C) It is a web application for managing robots and their automation capabilities.

D) It is a tool for creating and managing automated workflows.

Explanation:

Answer – C

UiPath Orchestrator is a web application that enables the user to manage robots in executing repetitive business processes. It manages the resources used in automation projects and consumed by robots, and provides access to them through support for hierarchical structuring combined with fine-grained role assignment. Its power comes from its capability of managing the user's entire robot fleet. In Orchestrator, the user can define and assign roles, configure the automation capabilities of their accounts, and control the level of access a user should have. The user can also manage accounts, roles, permissions, users, and resources through the Orchestrator web application.

Don't miss out!

Visit the website below and you can sign up to receive emails whenever Exam OG publishes a new book. There's no charge and no obligation.

https://books2read.com/r/B-A-CUWW-OMCHC

BOOKS 2 READ

Connecting independent readers to independent writers.

Also by Exam OG

Microsoft Azure Fundamentals Exam AZ-900 Certification Concept Based Practice Question Latest Edition 2023
Case Based Practice Questions for Microsoft Azure Fundamentals Exam AZ-900 Certification - First Edition
Concept Based Practice Questions for Tableau Desktop Specialist Certification Latest Edition 2023
Concept Based Practice Questions for Salesforce Administrator Certification Latest Edition 2023
Practice Questions For Salesforce Administrator Certification Cased Based – Latest Edition
Concept Based Practice Questions for AWS Solutions Architect Certification Latest Edition 2023
AWS Solutions Architect Certification Case Based Practice Questions Latest Edition 2023
Concept Based Practice Questions for UiPath RPA Associate Certification Latest Edition 2023
Practice Questions for UiPath Certified RPA Associate Case Based
Concept Based Practice Question for Blue Prism in Robotic Process Automation (RPA)
Blue Prism Developer Certification Case Based Practice Question - Latest 2023
Blue Prism Professional Developer Certification Case Based Practice Questions - Latest Edition 2023
Practice Questions for Tableau Desktop Specialist Certification Case Based

Practice Questions for Snowflake Snowpro Core Certification Concept Based - Latest Edition 2023

www.ingramcontent.com/pod-product-compliance
Ingram Content Group UK Ltd.
Pitfield, Milton Keynes, MK11 3LW, UK
UKHW021656190726
13853UKWH00001B/296

9 798215 020241